A DAY IN AN ECOSYSTEM

24 HOURS IN THE WETLANDS

VIRGINIA SCHOMP

Cavendish Square
New York

Published in 2014 by Cavendish Square Publishing, LLC
303 Park Avenue South, Suite 1247, New York, NY 10010

Copyright © 2014 by Cavendish Square Publishing, LLC

First Edition

Website: cavendishsq.com

This publication represents the opinions and views of the author based on his or her personal experience, knowledge, and research. The information in this book serves as a general guide only. The author and publisher have used their best efforts in preparing this book and disclaim liability rising directly or indirectly from the use and application of this book.

CPSIA Compliance Information: Batch #WS13CSQ

All websites were available and accurate when this book was sent to press.

Library of Congress Cataloging-in-Publication Data
Schomp, Virginia.
24 hours in the wetlands / Virginia Schomp.
p. cm. — (a day in an ecosystem)
Includes bibliographical references and index.
Summary: "Take a look at what takes place within a 24-hour period in the wetlands. Learn firsthand about the features, plant life, and animals of the habitat"—Provided by publisher.
ISBN 978-1-60870-897-0 (hardcover) ISBN 978-1-62712-070-8 (paperback)
ISBN 978-1-60870-904-5 (ebook)
1. Wetlands—Juvenile literature. I. Title. II. Title: Twenty four hours in the wetlands.
QH87.3.S39 2013
551.41—dc23
2011041776

Editor: Peter Mavrikis
Art Director: Anahid Hamparian
Series Designer: Kay Petronio
Photo research by Alison Morretta

Printed in the United States of America

CONTENTS

DAWN

THE MORNING sun lights up a vast field of grass. The ground beneath your feet feels soft and squishy. What is this soggy place? You are in the Florida Everglades. The Everglades is one of the world's largest **wetlands**.

It is easy to see how wetlands got their name. They are lands that are soaked or covered with shallow water. Some wetlands are as small as a wading pool. Some are bigger than a country. The waters may be still or moving, fresh or salty. The ground may be wet all the time or for just a few weeks a year. All these different conditions mean that there are many kinds of wetlands. A chilly **marsh** in Alaska, a steamy **swamp** in Brazil, a muddy **bog** in England—each has its own special features, but they are all wetlands.

Each type of wetland has its own living things, too. Mosses cover bogs like a soft, spongy carpet. Small grasshoppers and tall moose munch

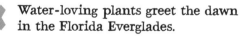
Water-loving plants greet the dawn in the Florida Everglades.

THE LAND OF GRASSY WATERS

The Seminole Indians of southern Florida called their lands Pa-hay-okee. That means "grassy waters." Early English explorers came up with another name. They saw fields of tall grass that seemed to stretch on forever. An English word for an open grassy place is *glade*. Aha! The Everglades!

on marsh grasses. Alligators and crocodiles hunt among the trees in swamp waters. Altogether, thousands of different types of plants and animals live in wetlands. Many of these **species** are found nowhere else on earth. No wonder wetlands are sometimes called "nurseries of life."

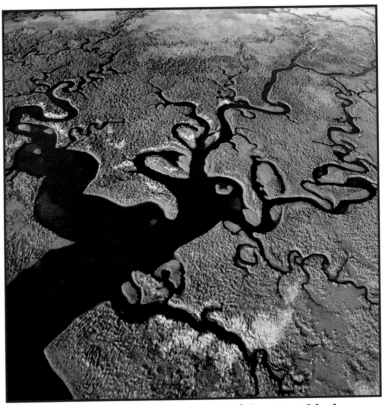

From the air, the Everglades are a wilderness of lush gardens and winding waterways.

Today you will explore one of these living nurseries. The Everglades cover more than 4,000 square miles (10,000 square kilometers) in southern Florida. The bottom half of this huge region is a public park. There are at least nine types of wetlands in Everglades National Park. Each holds an amazing assortment of plants and animals. So put on your wading boots. It is time to meet the living things that make their home in the wild and wet Everglades.

FIND THAT WETLAND!

This book explores nine different types of wetlands. See if you can spot them all on your adventure in the Everglades.

Freshwater marsh

Marl prairie

Slough

Pineland

Hardwood hammock

Cypress dome

Mangrove swamp

Salt marsh

Estuary

MORNING

WADING BOOTS—check. Hat, sunscreen, map—check. Warm coat and mittens—don't need them! It is late January, but the weather is fine in the Everglades. There are two seasons here, a hot "wet season" from May to November and a mild "dry season" from December to April. The dry season is a great time to visit. It is not too hot or rainy. There are fewer pesky mosquitoes. And the wild wetland creatures are easy to spot as they gather around the shrinking waterholes.

It is never a good idea to explore the wetlands alone. Luckily, you will not have to look far for company. A group of scientists have come to study a bird called the wood stork. Once, thousands of pairs of wood storks lived in the Everglades. By 1995, there were only five hundred pairs left. The scientists hope to find ways to help these birds and other **endangered species**.

◀ A wood stork perches on a cypress tree in an Everglades marsh.

Your adventure begins in a freshwater marsh. You and your scientist friends hike along a trail past fields of saw grass. Saw grass is not really a grass. It belongs to a group of grasslike plants called **sedges**. This tall sedge is named for the tiny ridges along the edges of the leaves. Watch your hands! Those sharp leaves can give you a nasty cut, like a paper cut.

Peek through the saw grass and you will see patches of ground. The marsh was covered with shallow water in the wet season. Now the water levels are dropping. But the ground will not dry out completely. The saw

Saw grass thrives in soil that is wet or flooded for most of the year.

grass marsh sits over a thick layer of **peat**. Peat is a kind of soil formed from decaying plants. It holds on to water like a sponge. The waterlogged soil will help the plants survive through the dry season.

Marshes can also form over a claylike soil known as marl. Marl marshes are often called **marl prairies**. A variety of plants grow in the marl prairie. You may see grasses, rushes, and bright wildflowers mixed in with the saw grass. Brownish mats of **periphyton** cover the bare ground between plants. Periphyton is made up of **algae.** During the wet season, the tiny algae plants clumped together in the water. As the marsh dried out, the plants died. The mats of dead algae settled to the ground. There they will provide food and shelter for insects and other small creatures.

The trail leads to a wooden boardwalk. Now you can keep your feet dry as you walk over the

YUCKY, YUMMY PERIPHYTON

Periphyton may look yucky, but it is an important part of marsh life. Many small wetland creatures munch on the dead algae. Insects, fish, and frogs lay their eggs in the moist mats. Periphyton also helps build up the marsh. As the algae decay, they form new layers of marl soil.

A wooden walkway crosses the flooded lands of Taylor Slough.

slough. Sloughs are the deepest part of the marsh. They are flooded with 1 to 3 feet (30 to 90 centimeters) of water for at least 11 months of the year.

There are two sloughs in the Everglades. You are looking out over narrow Taylor Slough. Shark River Slough to the west is wider and longer. Both sloughs are crowded with tall stands of saw grass. It is easy to see why the Everglades have been called the "River of Grass."

River is a good name for a slough, because the water does not stand still. Instead, it moves . . . very . . . very . . . slowly. The sloughs carry water from central Florida through the Everglades. They wander south through sunny marshes and shady swamps. They bring life-giving water to the plants and animals. At last, the marshy rivers reach the southern tip of Florida, where they empty into Florida Bay.

⌒

The River of Grass is not *all* grass. In some parts of the slough, other plants have elbowed out the saw grass. Spikerush and cattails stand in the shallow water near shore. White water lilies and yellow spatterdock float on the deeper water. Some plants grow completely underwater. Can you see them waving in the gentle current? The mermaid weed has feathery reddish brown leaves. The stems of the coontail look like little green raccoon tails.

All these wetland plants face different challenges than plants that grow on dry land. Can you guess their biggest problem? Too much water! Plants need **oxygen** to survive, but there is not

A **rodent** called a capybara in the Pantanal

THE GREAT PANTANAL

The Pantanal of Brazil is the largest wetland in the world. It gets its water from dozens of rivers. In the rainy season, the rivers overflow. The wetland spreads out over more than 96,000 square miles (250,000 square kilometers). That makes the Pantanal bigger than all five Great Lakes combined.

AIR IN, AIR OUT

Plants make their own oxygen during **photosynthesis.** So why does a plant need to get oxygen from the air, soil, or water? Photosynthesis depends on sunlight. When the sun is out, plants give off extra oxygen through their leaves. At night, photosynthesis stops. Then plants must take some of their oxygen back.

Spatterdock is a wetlands plant with floating leaves and small yellow flowers.

much room for oxygen in soil soaked with water. The plants you see here had to develop ways to get enough oxygen. These **adaptations** help each plant survive in its part of the wetlands.

Take a look at the cattail stems. They are long and hollow. These tall plants take in oxygen from the air. The oxygen passes down through the stems to the roots buried in the wet soil.

Water lilies are rooted in deeper water. A long, stretchy stem connects the roots to the leaves floating on the surface. The stems and leaves are filled with air spaces. That lets oxygen travel down from the leaves to the parts underwater. The trapped air also helps floating plants stay afloat.

What about the mermaid weed and coontail? Plants that live underwater have lots of small, thin leaves. The leaves do not have a protective covering like the waxy coat on most land leaves. That lets these plants absorb oxygen right from the water.

AFTERNOON

IT IS NOON—time for lunch! Your friends have brought some sandwiches. Eat fast! Otherwise, you might end up sharing your meal with a hungry ant or horsefly.

Thousands of insects crawl, hop, and fly through the Everglades. These wild lands are also home to large numbers of fish, birds, and other animals. Every one of these creatures depends on the others to survive. Each living thing needs water, soil, heat, and sunlight. Together, all the living and nonliving parts of this wet world make up the Everglades **ecosystem**.

An anhinga dives into the slough. The glossy black bird disappears beneath the sunlit surface. Wait . . . wait . . . . There! The bird pops back up. It has speared a big catfish with its long, pointed beak.

A pointed beak and long neck make the anhinga an expert fisherman.

A colorful **purple gallinule** feeds on a spatterdock fruit.

The dry season is the best time for bird-watching in the Everglades. As the marshes dry out, fish crowd the lasting waters of the slough. The all-you-can-eat buffet attracts flocks of fish-eating birds. You can see great blue herons, white ibis, snowy egrets, and other long-legged wading birds in the water. Some of the birds live here year-round. Others fly down from the chilly north to spend a cozy winter in Florida.

Fish are not the only food in the slough. Listen! Do you hear that squeaky call? A purple gallinule is looking for fruits, seeds, and insects. Look up! A short-tailed hawk soars overhead. It swoops down to capture a smaller bird. This winged hunter also feeds on mice, frogs, and lizards.

The slough attracts other **predators**, too. Do you see that gray bump in the water? An American alligator is spying on the anhinga. The bird flies back to its nest in a branch over the water. Three fluffy white chicks bob their heads and beg for some catfish. The alligator watches quietly. It waits for one of the eager babies to fall out of the nest. No luck this time. So the hungry **reptile** swims off in search of a fat fish or turtle.

How does the anhinga swim underwater? Why do herons have such long legs and necks? Just like the plants, the birds of the Everglades have adaptations that help them make the most of life in the wetlands.

Most waterbirds have special glands that coat their feathers with waterproof oil. The anhinga has no oil glands. When this bird dives, its feathers get soaked. The wet, heavy feathers help it swim low in the water. After the anhinga leaves the water, it spreads its wings to dry in the sun.

You saw how the anhinga spears its food. Herons can use their pointy beaks the same way. Watch the great blue heron hunting in the slough. With its long legs, it can wade out to the deepest water. The bird stands still as a statue. Suddenly, its long neck shoots out. It stabs down into the water and comes up with a spotted sunfish.

Other birds are adapted for other kinds of food. The ibis has a long downturned beak. That lets it

A northern shoveler

ALASKA'S WETLAND HOMES

Wetlands cover nearly half of Alaska. That means plenty of living space for waterbirds. This northern shoveler spends the summer feasting on plants and insects in an Alaskan marsh. In the fall, the big-beaked duck heads south. It may fly thousands of miles to reach its warm winter grounds in the Everglades.

poke deep into the mud, where crabs and crayfish hide. The avocet's long beak curves up. This bird probes for insects and other small creatures scurrying around near the surface. The hawk uses its strong, curved claws to catch its **prey**. Its hooked beak is the perfect tool for tearing into a meal.

All these different adaptations are the reason so many types of birds can live together in the wetlands. One bird may eat fish, while another prefers bugs or plants. Some find their meals near the surface, others deep in the water, and still others along the shore. No need to fight! With

A white ibis uses its long, curved beak to search for a snack.

so many different tastes, there is plenty of food here for all.

❧

Take a peek in the reeds. An American bittern is hiding there, but you may have a hard time seeing it. This bird is a master of **camouflage**. When it feels threatened, it stands with its beak pointing up. The bird sways slowly from side to side. The brown and white stripes on its throat and breast make it look like reeds waving in the breeze.

Camouflage helps the bittern hide from hungry predators. But this kind of adaptation can work for hunters, too. Remember the alligator? Its bumpy gray skin made it look like a rock or log in the water. That disguise helps the alligator sneak up on its prey.

Other adaptations add to this predator's powers. The alligator's strong jaws can crunch through even a hard turtle shell. Its long, muscular tail makes it a fast swimmer. Its eyes and nostrils are on top of its head, so it can hunt with only a small part of its

THE GALLINULE'S BOOTS

The purple gallinule's feet look like weird yellow rain boots. Those "boots" are an adaptation to life in the wetlands. The bird uses its long toes to spread its weight over the surface of floating plants. That lets the gallinule walk where most other birds have to swim.

Dark gray skin helps this toothy alligator blend in with its watery surroundings.

body showing. The gator even has a pair of "swim goggles." When it dives, a clear eyelid covers each eye so that it can see underwater.

You might think the world would be better off without this scary predator. Think again! The alligator is one of the most important animals in the Everglades ecosystem. An adult gator uses its snout and claws to dig out its own swimming hole. When the marsh dries out, the gator hole may be one of the few places left with water. Fish, frogs, insects, snakes, and turtles move in. Birds, raccoons, deer, and other animals stop by for a drink.

All these animals do not use the gator hole for free. Once in a while, the alligator collects "rent." One good meal can last it a week. In return, the water in the gator hole helps the wetland creatures survive the long dry season.

EVENING

YOU LEAVE THE boardwalk to hike along a wooded trail. You have come to a part of the Everglades called the **pineland**. The pineland is drier than the marsh. Forests of tall slash pine trees thrive in the rocky soil. Slash pines need soil that is wet but not *too* wet. A short flood is fine, but the roots cannot get enough oxygen if the ground stays wet too long.

These trees need something else to survive—fire. Every few years, a lightning strike sets off a wildfire in the dry pineland. The thick bark of the slash pines protects them from the flames. Thin-skinned **hardwood trees** burn up in the fire. That keeps the hardwoods from growing too tall and blocking the light that baby pines need to grow.

A black and yellow zebra butterfly flutters over a flower. A red-bellied woodpecker drums on a pine tree. The bird spots a rat snake winding

◀ Tall slash pines grow in some of the driest parts of the Everglades.

its way up the trunk. With a loud rattling call, the woodpecker flaps off in search of a safer perch.

The pinelands provide food and shelter to many wetland creatures. Butterflies feed on the sweet plant **nectar**. Birds build their nests in the trees. Some birds dine on the pineland seeds, nuts, fruits, and insects. Others fly to a nearby marsh to catch fish, snails, and other water creatures.

Snakes have their pick of food, too. The rat snake will climb as high as it takes to raid a nest of bird eggs or hatchlings. Down in the underbrush, eastern coral snakes and scarlet snakes hunt for frogs and lizards.

Watch your step! The coral snake is dangerous. Its bold red, yellow, and black rings are a warning sign: KEEP AWAY! I AM POISONOUS! The scarlet king snake has the same colors but no poison. This snake kills by squeezing its prey. Its copycat colors are a trick to scare off larger predators.

This harmless scarlet king snake has the same colors as its poisonous cousin the coral snake.

The woods around you get thicker and darker. The pine needles give way to broad green leaves. What is this lush jungle? You are walking through a **hardwood hammock**. Hammocks are small forests of leafy trees that grow where the ground rises a few inches. These "tree islands" are scattered throughout the Everglades. There are hammocks in pinelands, marshes, and swamps.

Some of the hammock trees may look familiar. You can see oaks, maples, and other trees often found in cooler lands up north. There are also **tropical** trees such as mahogany, royal palm, and gumbo limbo. All these trees sit above the floods during the wet season. The hammock is also protected from wildfires. Water forms a ring around the tree island, like a moat around a castle.

Mammals come to the hammock for food or a drink at the moat. You can see some of their tracks in the muddy ground. A white-tailed deer left the heart-shaped hoofprints. The small doglike tracks were made by

An oak tree spreads its branches in a hardwood hammock.

The endangered Florida panther

BIG, FIERCE . . . AND SHY

The Florida panther is a fierce predator. It hunts deer, wild pigs, and raccoons. It may even attack an alligator. But this big cat is also shy. It needs large wilderness areas to survive. When people clear the land to build houses and shopping malls, the panther loses its home.

a gray fox. The black bear's tracks look like a human footprint with claws.

What about those big rounded tracks with four toes? They belong to a Florida panther. You would have to be very lucky to see one of these big cats. Years ago, panthers lived all over the southeastern United States. Today there are only about one hundred wild panthers left.

It is getting late, and your legs are getting tired. Why not hop a ride? A park ranger is driving down the main park road. There is just enough room for you and your friends in the car.

You drive past marl prairies dotted with dwarf cypress trees. These marshy lands are flooded for a few months each year. The trees cannot grow tall because the soil is too shallow and poor in **nutrients**.

Here and there, a **cypress dome** rises above the dwarfs. Cypress domes are small, round forests. They form in spots where the water is deeper and the soil is richer than in the surrounding prairie. The tallest cypress trees grow in the deepest water, at the center of the dome. Smaller trees grow around the edges.

A walk through a cypress dome can be fun, if you don't mind getting your feet wet. Wading birds nest in the trees. Fish, snakes, and turtles swim in the pools of water. *Shhh!* You will want to walk quietly past the alligator hole!

The ranger drops you off near Paurotis Pond. Every winter, wading birds fly in from all over the Everglades to raise their young here. Herons, egrets, and ibis wade in the still, shallow water. A cormorant basks in the sun. A spoonbill fluffs up its pink feathers. But the bird that really stands out is the one you have come all this way to see— the endangered wood stork.

Wood storks have bald black heads and white feathers with black tips. They gather in large nesting colonies around the start of the dry

Spanish moss, a type of epiphyte

UP IN THE AIR

Epiphytes, or "air plants," cling to the trees in the cypress dome. The plants wrap their roots around a trunk or branch. That gives them a place to live above the shady forest floor. Air plants get their water and nutrients from the rain and air.

Wood stork parents keep close watch over their growing chicks.

season. A pair of storks builds a nest on a tree island in the pond. The female lays two to five eggs. About a month later, the eggs hatch. The chicks look like small fuzzy copies of the adults. For the next eight or nine weeks, they will depend on their parents for food and protection.

The scientists have set up their telescopes. You focus on a stork wading in the pond. The bird finds its food by touch. It sweeps its open beak back and forth in the muddy water. When it feels a fish, it snaps its beak shut. How fast is this fisherman? The time from touch to snap is just one-fortieth of a second.

The wood stork flies back to the nest with its catch. The chicks bob their heads and cry out for their share. These babies need a lot of food to grow quickly. By the time a young stork flies off on its own, it will have eaten about 35 pounds (16 kilograms) of food. That is a lot of fish—and a lot of work for the busy parents!

The sun is sinking. The scientists pack up their equipment. They have counted the stork nests. They have watched the parents fishing and feeding the chicks. When they get back home, they will write a report. They will combine what they have learned with findings from other studies.

In those studies, scientists have looked at stork nesting grounds from airplanes, by boat, and on the ground. They have tested the water. They have found out when wood storks build their nests, what they feed their young, and how fast the young birds grow.

Studies like these have helped scientists understand why the number of wood storks is dropping. When people build on or near wetlands, they change the way the water flows. The ponds near stork nesting grounds may get too shallow or too deep. There may not be enough fish to raise a family of growing chicks.

Studies also tell us what these birds need to survive. Scientists can use that information to come up with plans for protecting nesting sites and restoring the wetlands.

NESTING TIME

Wood storks build their nests at the start of the dry season. That way, they can be sure there will be enough food for their growing families. During the rainy season, the wetlands flood. Large fish multiply in the waters. When the rains stop, the land dries out and fish crowd together in the shrinking ponds. That makes easy pickings for a bird that hunts by touch.

NIGHT

IT IS A LONG walk back to the park entrance. No worries! The scientists have two canoes waiting. They invite you to join them on a nighttime paddle. The trip will take you all the way to the end of the Everglades.

As you push off, a flock of snow-white egrets flaps into the sunset. The birds will spend the night resting high up in a hardwood hammock. Other daytime creatures are settling down to sleep, too. But that does not mean the wetlands are silent. All around you, frogs and toads are tuning up for their nightly chorus. A raccoon waddles off to its favorite fishing hole. A hungry bobcat crouches near the entrance to a rabbit den. These **nocturnal** creatures rested during the day. At night, they will haunt the dark wetlands with their strange calls and quiet rustlings.

◄ Birds fly to their nighttime roosts on a small island in Florida Bay.

The snapping turtle has powerful jaws for catching prey and keeping safe from other predators.

The canoe trail winds through a grassy marsh. Shine your flashlight and you might catch sight of a pig frog. A piglike grunt tells you how this big green frog got its name.

The leopard frog's call sounds like a chuckle. This spotted frog is a champion jumper. When it sees your light, it flies through the air and vanishes in the water.

That mighty leap can help the leopard frog catch a tasty water bug. The frog will also jump to escape a Florida snapping turtle. The turtle has strong, sharp jaws for snapping up frogs, fish, mice, and birds. It hunts in the shallow water. Its mud-colored shell acts as camouflage, helping the snapper surprise its prey.

Both frogs and turtles must watch out for larger predators. Raccoons have sharp hearing and night vision for tracking down mice and rats. The opossum finds its prey with its keen sense of smell. Water snakes use their forked tongue to hunt. When a snake flicks its tongue, it is "tasting" the air to figure out the direction of a smell.

The marshes give way to tall mangrove trees. These hardy trees are a sign that you are getting near the coast. Mangroves thrive where freshwater from the Everglades mixes with salt water from the sea.

You will have to paddle slowly through the mangrove swamp. The red mangroves send out a tangle of "prop roots." These tall, arching roots keep the trees from toppling over in the muddy soil. They also help the

The long roots of red mangrove trees have special cells that filter out salt from the water.

THE STINKY SWAMP

The first thing you might notice about the mangrove swamp is not the trees. It is the smell! There is little oxygen in the thick mud. The tiny **bacteria** that live there breathe **sulfur** instead. These bacteria do an important job. They break down the dead vegetation and release the nutrients into the soil and water. They also give off a sulfur gas that smells like—*phew!*—rotten eggs.

mangroves breathe. The parts above the surface send oxygen down to the parts under the water.

The mangrove swamp may look deserted, but it is actually bursting with life. Snails, crabs, shrimp, and crayfish live among the tangled web of roots. Fish lay their eggs in the flooded forest. Wading birds nest in the branches and feed in the muddy water.

Only the nocturnal birds are out now. A barred owl sounds an eerie *hoo-hoo-too-HOO!* It is sitting on a high branch, looking and listening. Its big ears pick up the faint rustle of a rat. *Swoosh!* The owl dives down and snatches up its snack.

Your canoe scrapes bottom as you reach the **salt marsh**. The ground is dry now, but this low-lying area is often flooded with seawater. Tropical storms and hurricanes bring high winds and ocean waves. Even mangroves cannot survive in these harsh conditions. Instead of trees, the salt marsh is covered with low-growing grasses, sedges, and shrubs.

One of the scientists plucks a leaf from a saltwort shrub. You take a bite. It tastes like a salty pickle! These marsh plants are adapted to growing in salty soil. Saltwort gets rid of extra salt through tiny openings in its leaves. Other plants have special roots that take in water but block the salt.

Be sure to keep your flashlight on as you hike through the dark marsh. An American crocodile may be lying beside the trail. The crocodile eats fish,

Saltwort and other hardy plants grow in the salty soil near the coast.

crabs, turtles, and just about anything else that moves. It is shy around people. If you get too close, it will probably splash into the water and swim away. Still, you will want to keep out of the way of this toothy reptile!

Many smaller creatures spend their lives in the salty water. Snails feed on the algae growing on the mud and grasses. Clams, oysters, and fiddler crabs filter tiny bits of food from the water. When the tide rises, fish swim through the flooded marsh. Diamondback terrapins paddle around, hunting for fish, crabs, and snails. The turtles get freshwater by drinking rain and dew from the leaves and ground. A terrapin may even take a sip of rainwater from another turtle's back.

The trail opens up into a muddy beach. A soft light glows on a large body of water. It is nearly sunrise, and you have reached the shores of Florida Bay. The bay is an **estuary**—a sheltered place where freshwater flows into the ocean. Here the waters from the Everglades sloughs meet the sea.

You wade out into the shallow water. The muddy bottom is covered with algae and sea grasses. A host of fish and shellfish live and feed in this underwater city. Many use the bay as a nursery. The young sea creatures take shelter among the grasses until they are ready to move out into the open ocean.

A chain of green islands encloses Florida Bay. Seabirds rest on the islands at night and return to the bay in the morning. A few early birds are on their way now. That swift-moving cloud is a flock of snowy egrets. Gulls swoop in with their noisy, laughing calls. A brown pelican plunges headfirst into the water. When it pops back up, its stretchy throat pouch is filled with fish.

The sun peeks out over the water. Fishermen launch their boats into the golden streak of light. Nearly a million people come to the Everglades each year to enjoy the water and wildlife. They fish in the bays. They hike the trails. They paddle through flooded forests and seas of grass.

The Everglades are more than just a fun place to visit. Wetlands give us many other gifts, too. They store rainwater and slowly release it into our rivers and underground pools. They help clean the water by filtering out waste and pollution. Mangrove swamps and salt marshes protect our

Side views of a crocodile (top) and an alligator

SMILE, CROCODILE!

Alligators and crocodiles are cousins. Can you tell these two reptiles apart? The alligator has a wide, rounded snout. When its jaws are closed, you cannot see its lower teeth. The croc's snout is longer and more pointed. Two huge teeth stick up from its lower jaw. So remember: If you see a toothy smile, you have met a crocodile.

Brown pelicans in the Florida Everglades

WORKING TOGETHER

Fifty years ago, brown pelicans nearly died out. Farmers were using a **pesticide** called DDT on their crops. DDT washed off the land into the water. When pelicans ate fish from the water, the poison got into their bodies. They laid eggs with thin shells, which burst before hatching. Then DDT was banned. Today thousands of pelicans soar over our coasts once again.

coastlines from storm winds and waves. Wetlands are a source of food, building materials, and other products for people. They are home to millions of plants and animals.

The sun rises over the sheltered waters of Florida Bay.

But this important ecosystem is in trouble. More than half of the world's wetlands have been lost. People have drained the water to make way for houses, roads, and farms. Wetlands have also been damaged by pesticides used on farms, chemicals used in factories, and oil spills at sea.

Today we know that a healthy world depends on healthy wetlands. Scientists are learning more about wetlands and the plants and animals that live there. Conservation groups are working to stop wetland losses. Governments around the world are taking steps to protect and restore their wetlands. That is good news for the endangered wood storks and Florida panthers. It is good news for us all.

Polluted water from farms and factories can harm wetland plants and animals.

WHERE ARE THE WETLANDS?

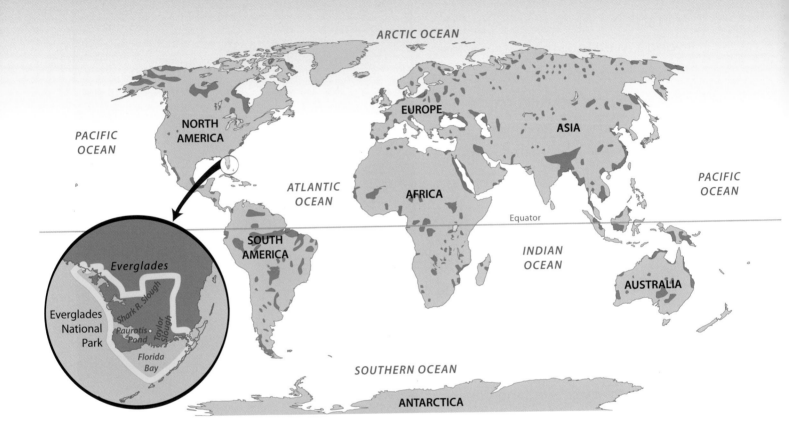

Wetlands cover about 6 percent of the world's land surface. This map shows the location of the major wetlands.

FAST FACTS ABOUT WETLANDS AND THE FLORIDA EVERGLADES

LOCATION: Wetlands are found all over the world, except in Antarctica. The Everglades are located in southern Florida.

SIZE: Wetlands come in many different sizes, from a few square feet to thousands of acres. The Everglades cover about 4,000 square miles (10,000 square kilometers).

TEMPERATURE: Wetland temperatures vary depending on the place, season, and time of day. In the Everglades, the temperatures average about 80 degrees Fahrenheit (27 degrees Celsius) in the summer and about 70°F (21°C) in the winter.

RAINFALL: The amount of rainfall in wetlands varies, depending on the place and season. The Everglades average about 60 inches (150 centimeters) of water a year.

PLANTS FOUND IN THE EVERGLADES include trees, shrubs, grasses, sedges, rushes, ferns, orchids, mosses, floating plants such as water lilies, submerged plants such as coontail, and air plants such as butterfly orchids.

ANIMALS FOUND IN THE EVERGLADES: *Amphibians* include pig frogs, southern leopard frogs, and eastern spadefoot toads. *Birds* include American avocets, American bitterns, anhingas, bald eagles, barred owls, black-crowned night herons, brown pelicans, double-crested cormorants, great blue herons, roseate spoonbills, purple gallinules, red-bellied woodpeckers, short-tailed hawks, snail kites, snowy egrets, white ibis, and wood storks. *Fish* include bass, catfish, gar, killifish, minnows, sunfish, and tarpon. *Insects* include beetles, butterflies, dragonflies, grasshoppers, horseflies, and mosquitoes. *Mammals* include black bears, bobcats, cotton mice, Everglades minks, Florida panthers, gray foxes, marsh rabbits, North American raccoons, roof rats, white-tailed deer, and wild pigs. *Reptiles* include American alligators, American crocodiles, eastern coral snakes, scarlet king snakes, mangrove water snakes, yellow rat snakes, diamondback terrapins, and Florida snapping turtles. There are also many crabs, crayfish, lobsters, shrimp, clams, mussels, snails, sponges, worms, and spiders.

GLOSSARY

adaptations—Ways in which living things adapt, or change to survive under the conditions in a certain environment.

algae (AL-jee)—Simple plantlike organisms that live mostly in the water.

bacteria (back-TEER-ee-uh)—Simple living things made up of just one cell, which are usually too small to see without a microscope.

bog—A wetland that gets its water entirely from rainfall, where the soil is poor and peat builds up from the dead plants.

camouflage (KAM-uh-flaj)—Coloring or other physical features that help living things blend in with their surroundings, hiding them from other animals.

cypress dome—A small round forest of cypress trees that grows in a dome shape, with the tallest trees in the center and shorter trees around the edges.

ecosystem—An area that is home to a particular community of plants and animals, which are specially suited to living in that environment. An ecosystem includes all the living things of the area plus all the nonliving things, such as the water, soil, and rocks.

endangered species—Plants and animals that are in danger of becoming extinct, or dying out completely.

epiphytes (EH-puh-fites)—Plants that grow on other plants, instead of in the ground. Epiphytes are also called air plants.

estuary (ES-chuh-wer-ee)—A partly enclosed body of water where freshwater from the land meets salt water from the sea.

hardwood hammock—An "island" of hardwood trees growing on an elevated site surrounded by lower, wetter land.

hardwood trees—Trees with broad leaves, such as oaks and maples. The wood is sometimes but not always harder than the wood of softwood trees such as pines.

mammals—Animals that are warm-blooded, breathe air, and nurse their young with milk.

marl prairies (marl PRAIR-eez)—Marshes that form over marl, a gray, crumbly soil made up mostly of clay.

marsh—A wetland that is saturated or flooded for much of the year, where grasses and grasslike plants grow in the rich soil.

nectar—A sweet liquid made by flowers.

nocturnal—Active mainly at night.

nutrients (NOO-tree-uhnts)—Substances that are taken in by plants and animals to help them live and grow.

oxygen (AHK-sih-jun)—An element that is found in the air and water. Almost all living things need oxygen to survive.

peat—A kind of soil made up of the remains of partially decayed plants.

periphyton (puh-RIH-fuh-tahn)—Thick brownish mats made up of different types of algae and other tiny organisms.

pesticide—A chemical used to kill insects or weeds.

photosynthesis (foe-toe-SIN-thuh-sus)—The process by which plants use the energy from sunlight to combine water and carbon dioxide to make food. Photosynthesis also produces oxygen.

pineland—An area covered mainly by pine trees.

predators—Animals that hunt and kill other animals for food.

prey—An animal that is hunted by a predator.

reptile—An animal that has scaly skin and, in most cases, lays eggs.

rodent—A small animal with big front teeth for gnawing.

salt marsh—A marsh that forms along the coast, where freshwater and salt water mix together.

sedges—Tall grasslike plants with triangular stems, which are common in wetlands.

slough (sloo)—A shallow, slow-moving river that channels water through a wetland.

species (SPEE-sheez)—Specific types of plants and animals.

sulfur—A pale yellow element that occurs widely in nature.

swamp—A wetland that is saturated or flooded for much of the year, where trees and shrubs grow in the rich soil.

tropical—Found in the tropics, the warm region just north and south of the earth's equator.

wetlands—Areas of land where the ground is saturated or covered with shallow water for all or part of the year.

FIND OUT MORE

Books

Benoit, Peter. *Wetlands*. New York: Children's Press, 2011.

Johansson, Philip. *Marshes and Swamps: A Wetland Web of Life*. Berkeley Heights, NJ: Enslow, 2008.

Kirkland, Jane. *Take a Wetlands Walk*. Lionville, PA: Stillwater Publishing, 2008.

Sturm, Jeanne. *Restoring Wetlands*. Vero Beach, FL: Rourke Publishing, 2010.

Watson, Galadriel. *Wetlands*. New York: Weigl Publishers, 2011.

Websites

Biomes of the World: Wetlands

www.mbgnet.net/fresh/wetlands/index.htm

Follow the links to learn about freshwater wetlands and some of the animals that live in them. This colorful site is presented by the Missouri Botanical Garden.

Everglades National Park: Natural Features and Ecosystems

www.nps.gov/ever/naturescience/naturalfeaturesandecosystems.htm

Learn about the natural features, plants, and animals of the Everglades at this National Park Service website.

Friends of the Everglades

http://everglades.org/young-friends/educational-resources/

Click on the links for games, activity sheets, and other materials for learning more about the Everglades.

Wetlands

www.nwrc.usgs.gov/wetlands/wetlandsInfo.htm

This National Wetlands Research Center site offers information and photos relating to different types of wetlands.

INDEX

Page numbers in **boldface** are illustrations.

ABOUT THE AUTHOR

VIRGINIA SCHOMP has written more than eighty books for young readers on topics including dinosaurs, dolphins, world history, American history, myths, and legends. She lives among the tall pines of New York's Catskill Mountain region. When she is not writing books, she enjoys hiking, gardening, baking (and eating!) cookies, watching old movies and new anime, and, of course, reading, reading, and reading.

PHOTO CREDITS